Teach Me How to Roar:

How to Become a Man Without a Father to Show You How

By

Lee Harden

Copyright © 2013

Cover design by Writer.ly Star Services

ISBN:0615898556
ISBN-13:978-0-615-89855-1

Dedication:

This novel is dedicated to my wife Cindy, my mother Augusta Harden, my "Finishing" father, JL Wilson, J.S., L.G., and the various members of my "Parenting Team" that contributed towards me being the man that I am today. My journey is not finished but without you I would have never made it to where I am as a man and a person that I am today. I love all of you.

Contents

Part II The Transformation

Part I My Story

Introduction

Absence. According to the internet the word "absence" means to be away from a place or person. The absence of parental figures can be devastating to many members of a family. The decisions that parents make can affect their children in many ways. But what do you do if one of your parents elects to not be a part of your life? How do you cope with that? For a young child that is now a full grown man that choice, that decision that my father has made has haunted me the majority of my life.

The relationship with my father that I craved was very toxic for me and learning how to balance my emotions and evolve and grow as a man was something that was both tragic and a triumph. I use the word tragic because my life is not the only life affected by my father's decisions. There is another generation that is affected by his chosen absence. The triumph in my story is the fact that I was able to become a grown man and I represent all of the things that is good about growing up and becoming everything that a positive role model should be. But that has its own negative aspect because my father does not know me and the man that I have become. The story in this book is two fold, the first half is my story. How I became the man that I am today and the people that helped me get to this point.

The second half of this story is how I eliminated the pain. But the pain never really goes away. It's muted and calmed, by managing your pain you can better understand how to move forward instead of focusing on the past. The great absence can be terrible. You feel alone and unwanted, the lack of love from the person that should love you the most is unbearable at times. But if you learn how to manage the absence, your life will change forever. That's why I am writing this book. I want mothers, sons, teachers, fathers, pastors, and friends to share this information with people that struggle with their absence. My transformation is still on going but I know who I am now. I know that my kingdom is at my feet and I must walk into my destiny with authority. Earlier in my life I did not know that my father was the king of the jungle I was just a cub. I did not know I would be a lion one day. I never saw my father get angry and I have never seen him preside over his kingdom.

I did not know my own power when I was younger and my voice was too small to be taken seriously. But now I know that I am a mighty lion and my kingdom lies before me and my strength is in my family and the people that I love. My voice that was once too small is now a mighty roar, a roar that I had to learn was inside me all along. My inner strength was being muted by the pain that I was carrying with me in my spirit for all of those years but not anymore. Learn how to break the connection that we carry with the struggles from our past. Learn how to heal. *Learn how YOU can roar like I did.*

The Little Box

The "Little Box" is what I believe all of the bad
things that I experience go. This place in my mind and
spirit is no longer the source of my hatred for my father and
all of the negative thoughts and experiences that I deposited
there during my youth. Now it serves a different purpose
and I will get into that later. I believe that all young people
keep their memories in a certain place in their heart and
that place is wonderful because you can revisit past
experiences and enjoy them as much as you want to. But
for me my memories of my time with my father and my
feelings for him are bittersweet.

My biological father and I had a good relationship
for a moment in my life. I actually spent a couple of years
with him and his family when I was 4 and 5 years old. I can
remember him taking me to get my hair cut and trips to
McDonald's afterwards for breakfast. I have great
memories of sitting on his lap and pretending like I was

driving his car (this is probably the reason why I love cars so much to this day). Things were truly great for me and him during the beginning of my life. He was married to another woman and she had a daughter who was around 5 to 6 years older than me. Their relationship seemed to be what I saw on television and even at a young age I wondered why he was not with my mother.

During the time that I was with my father my mother was back in Ohio getting her career going in preparation for me to come back to stay with her. Here is where the problems with me started, when my mom and I spoke on the phone, I felt so unhappy because she was not there with me. I began to cry a lot. At that time I guess I was a bit unstable. That brings me back to the "little box." For some reason I can't really remember too much of those years with my father. It seems like I put the majority of the things that I liked and did not like in that place and in essence deleted it out of my mind.

Now that I am writing this I am starting to remember some things about my life in Atlanta in 1980. Life was not that bad. I remember my father as a young, hard-working man. He worked as a driver for a local beer merchandiser and he was a good father. Surprisingly, my father was very protective; I never felt scared when I was staying with him. I liked the feeling of safety and comfort that his presence provided me.

Not that I did not feel the same way with my mother but it was *different* with my father. For me my father represented something that I think most grown men can speak to: he was something to copy and emulate. He was super strong, and in his youth he had muscles. He was not very tall--around six feet standing upright—but to me he was a giant and *I wanted to be just like him.*

My stepmother was nice to me for the most part, I never quite felt as important to her as her own daughter, which may explain why I gravitated towards my father so much. I remember having to sit at the table to eat my food during my picky eating phase; I also remember very vividly of the way she used to thump me in the head as a form of discipline. Don't get me wrong, it was not abuse or anything that severe but it was a thump to my forehead with her finger that is similar to the action a person would use to check the ripeness of a melon. This thumping was particularly disturbing to me; I did not like it at all. I remember resenting it, and I became sort of afraid of her. During my time away from my mother I can remember wishing she could join my father and me in Atlanta. I remember crying a lot. I don't know why I cried so much but I was very sad.

While I was with my father my mother was working on her career and she always planned on me returning to her. That would have been reassuring to know but I was too young to understand her desire to have me back over the telephone. Speaking of which, I should tell you about how telephone calls to my mother worked. I would talk to her and someone would always be on the phone with me-- either my father or his wife. This was weird to me but that type of behavior may be a small window into the future. At that point it was just strange. Did they not trust me being on the telephone by myself? Did they think that my mother was trying to get some information out of me? I don't know.

That is the beauty of the "little box." Things that bother me are instantly gone. I'm sure some psychiatrist has a term for what I am experiencing but to me it was a storage box, so to speak, for things that I did not want to be bothered with and that came with some unintended consequences.

I wonder how these experiences affected my young mind. I assume any damage may remain dormant (at least I hope it has) or something positive will manifest from writing this book. The way I was using my "little box" was a one-way thing; deposit only. There was supposed to be no way for things to get out of hand. But I was wrong. I was having problems dealing with my emotions. The problems started as I became a teenager. My father's absence created something in me that I can only describe as a dark place inside my spirit and inside that space was a bundle of negative energy filled with a rage that I cannot fully put into words.

This rage is nothing like who I am. It was a gross sense of contempt for my father and I hated him for not being there for me. This period in my life was like a rebirth, but in a bad way. My father's absence and the day-to-day bullying at school conceived a child that was not sure of himself, a child that did not believe in his intelligence, and all that translated onto the basketball court where I failed often and without a place to retreat. This made the school hallways pure hell. I remember several of the guys that I associated with making fun of me relentlessly. I could not speak up for myself, I did not understand who I was and I was holding my own self back on the basketball court. I had no outlet to work out the pain that I was feeling. I hated the fact that I had to go through those years at school. I felt like I would have been a better athlete if my father was in my life like some of my friend's fathers. This gave the "little box" more fuel and with that, my hatred grew.

The Pimple Years

School sucks sometimes, and kids can be A-holes. Yes, I said it. Some kids can be emotional piranha and that can lead to major issues. Bullying is real and going to school was significantly more difficult for me than it should have been. This is the part where I'm not sure how to assign blame. So I'll let you decide. When it came to school I was a decent student, I never really had any problems. I only got into one fight in the 3rd grade. But I never really felt like I was with the "in" crowd.

My best friend chased me home from school before we became buddies. These are just some of the "milder" events that occurred in my younger years around 3rd through5th grades. The tougher days were just around the corner.

I hated middle school; I hated everything associated with being a teenager. It was absolutely terrible. Teenage problems are universal but I felt I had issues that were unique to me. Let's start with the standard stuff: yes, I had bad skin and yes I was very awkward and gangly. And under most conditions that would be fine but here is the issue: at the time I was trying to create or should I say draw out of thin air a male identity that was separate from my mother, which is not very easy for someone to do, trust me. My mom had plenty of positive "role model type" men in my life to look up to but when it came time to press the copy button to create my own self identity, the sheet of paper that came out of the machine looked more pinkish than white. I was effeminate, soft spoken, and unsure of who I was. My fellow classmates tasted blood in the water and they were merciless. Years and years of being called "gay" and "fagot" rang in my ears. If I had only been the confident person I am now back then, I would go back in time and I'd right all of those situations. I'd be in a lot more fights but at least I would have stood up for myself.

For many years I did not have a girlfriend in middle school due to the social climate at my school and being associated with me no matter how tall I was would not be a good look for the most attractive and popular girls. So I was passed over even if secretly admired. Then there was sports, which is supposed to be the great equalizer if you had talent. Of which I did not, due to my lack of basketball skills compounded by my equally lacking levels of confidence. Mix all of those ingredients together and you have a recipe for a miserable adolescence, now with less sugar and tastier. I know, I can be a jerk but sometimes you have to just laugh at some things because if you didn't you would just want to die.   Thinking back at that time of my life I really should have told my mother what was going on at school. But she could not help me during this time of my life. I needed my father to help me cope with my anger.

Maybe he could have helped me be more comfortable talking to girls or maybe teach me how to fight? I never had to worry about someone trying to fight me because I was always so much taller than everyone else. I should have told someone at school about what the kids were doing to me but I was afraid of being labeled a "snitch" or something like that. So I just took it, years of the same people, treating me the same way. I know you are saying why didn't you just find new friends? Sports. Remember, I grew up and played with the same group of guys from 7th grade all the way through high school. If I played sports, I had to get it from the guys. All I wanted was acceptance but I did not have it from my male friends and I did not have it from my father either.

So what do I think is the cause of all of the misery during this important time period of my life? Is it really fair to blame someone that I barely know? Could a man really mean so much to my life that his absence during this time period could literally define my life? The answer to all of those questions is yes. The impact of my father's absence during this portion of my life is similar to a plane trying to from New York to Los Angles with only enough fuel for half of the distance. Sure I was okay but I could have been better off if my father was actively involved in my life. My mother did her absolute best to minimize the damage but this is something that "mommy" or in my case "Ma" could not fix. A couple of years ago I was thinking about this issue and I tried to categorize what specific parts of my life were affected by my father's absence. I think I figured it out.

Backspace Delete

If my father was at home with me and my mother I don't think I would have tolerated the name calling. My father did not play that mess. He is strong, and tough, he would have taught me how to stand up for myself and he would have not allowed me to let the bullying continue for as long as it did. I am not a violent person and neither is he. But I have his family's trademark temper and he would have taught me how to apply it in away that would convey strength without getting myself into too much trouble. Girls would not have been a problem either.

My father never had a problem with the ladies--at least, to my knowledge. Maybe if I had him with me I would have been more confident and comfortable in my own pimple laden, extremely long, and crackely voiced, skin. Sure being a teenager is tough for everyone but I can only speak for myself on this situation and I feel like things could have been better or at least minimized if he had a greater presence in my life. Sports would have also been better if I had him with me. We could have worked on my dribbling skills and my jump shot. During high school I grew six inches and finished at 6 feet 6 inches tall. Too bad I did not have the skills that my mom said I did not work hard enough for.

The truth is I hated playing basketball at my school for reasons already stated. I played AAU (Amateur Athletic Union) ball during my 11th grade year and I loved it because none of the guys I played with knew me. Wasted height? That's how I felt; maybe I was destined to be a writer. For a 12 year old your world is pretty limited, and you don't really know how you can add to society. Your goals are simple: get girls, get good grades, and stay on your mother's good side. But for me it was not that easy. I was not that simple. My life was more than just school; I still had to find out who the person was in the reflection of my bathroom mirror.

Mirror, Mirror on the Wall

"Who is this person that I am looking at?" That is what I used to say when I looked at myself in the bathroom mirror. Self-awareness is a b$%&#; you realize that the image that you see in the mirror is what others see when they see you, check. Then you realize that you, the physical you is in control of your arms and legs, check. Now you see your mortality right then and there. You control a body that will fail you and one day you will die.

Crap. That's pretty heavy for a teenager to realize especially when you have not figured out who the hell you are and that on its own is very frightening. So I had to realize that I am here, I did not know the reason. But it definitely was not to be a famous basketball player. I had to make myself comfortable with my own skin. I had to OWN my skin. It was not about self-awareness anymore it was about self-acceptance. Something had to change, I had to press the copy button again and hope that this time the sheet would be free of color. Again, there was no image. I needed ink.

The Engineer

I mentioned earlier that my single mother had men in her life that on occasion had the opportunity to meet me. This was a big deal for me because if you made it to dinner with me then the guy must really be special. One of these gentlemen was JL. I guess God put JL in my life to provide some form of buffer to all of the crap that I was going through. If I had to put his personality into words I would say he is the calmest person I have ever met. The phrase "quiet confidence" is what I would refer to if I had to describe him.

JL gave me something that my mom could not: he gave me a reference point. Our relationship to this day is very strong, yet different now that I am older. When I was younger I would call him all of the time to get his opinion on all of my stupid teenage ideas, goals, and aspirations and

he never shot my ideas down. He always listened....well.
He is probably the best listener in the world. His ears
should be the size of his head he listens so well. I
remember it was time for me to learn how to drive and I
had recently gotten my learners permit and he took me out
in my mom's car and just said "drive". I looked at him and
he gave me a confidence-inspiring half grin and I backed
my mom's Chevy Nova out of the parking space and drove.

No lessons really needed. His ability to gauge my
temperament is awesome, and that is one of the things that I
love about him. JL has also been a sounding board for both
my mom and me and when we don't see eye to eye on
issues and sometimes he was in between both of us and I
admit that was not fair to him. I used to get upset with him
secretly because I felt like if he lived with us my life would
have been easier and some of the issues that were
happening at school and carrying over at home would have
been minimized.

JL is an engineer by trade from one of the most famous African-American schools for engineering in the south. His approach to life seems to be based more on logic and common sense. I call it the "1+1=2" take on life. The difference between him and I is, I adhere to that principal firmly and he allows some variance or "grey" to my "black" and that difference between us is more rooted in the blood than our bond. Now I have some ink to use to create my new image.

My new identity can now be created based on lessons learned from a consistent example of what a man should be. How wonderful is this man to do this for me? I would not do it for someone else's child but he chose to do it for me. This brings me to a speed bump and a tough question that I had to ask myself. If JL enjoyed being my "finishing father" how come my real father did not want the job? Obviously, I was not a bad kid. I was relatively good so why would someone not want to be a father to me? JL's presence in my life was bittersweet, on one hand I have a man that is willing to by the "man prototype" in my life but at the same time he reminded me that there was another person who did not want the job. As an adult now and a father of two, I still think about this as my boys play with JL. More on that later.

Mr. H.

I want to clarify something to you. I do not want to give the wrong impression about my father. For the year or so that I stayed with him he was a great father to me. No question. During that time I had no doubts about how he felt about me. I was 4 going on 5 years old and he always made me feel safe and loved. He loves music and he would play his harmonica and listen to his records on the weekends. I remember him putting me on his lap and allowing me to steer the car while he was driving in a safe place in our neighborhood. That is a memory that I vividly remember to this day. I don't remember my father raising his voice with me. He might have had to discipline me a few times and that was enough. He also had that "quiet confidence".

Growing up as a teenager I desperately did not want to be like him. I tried my absolute best to not be like him and much to my surprise; there are some things that you just can't get away from. Genetics. I have his temper, I have his love of music and cars, I have his drive and ambition, and no matter what I do the blood bond (maybe that should be the name of this book) is too strong. I could not get away from him because he was a part of me. The good and the bad, to try to get away from him was impossible because I would be getting away from myself.

This really pissed me off and made my anger go nuclear. I would say to myself "I AM NOT HIM, I AM NOTHING LIKE HIM, <u>I WILL NOT BE LIKE HIM!</u>" I was saying all of that while speaking like him, shaving like him, being angry like him, and mirroring him in all kinds of ways even though I never lived with him extensively to learn this behavior. "You gotta be kidding me", I thought. I could not become this man. I had to accept that he is in me and declare that I was my own man, independent of my mother with my father's positive traits and shortcomings along with JL's influence sprinkled on top for flavor. Time to press the damn copy button. I saw an image this time on the paper when it came out of the machine. It was my reflection, I saw myself.

Great Balls of Fire

Now that I got myself figured out a bit, a marvelous thing happened in my life. High school. "Holy crap, this is great!" I thought. No more of the hell from middle school, I was at a new school with people that did not know all of my previous three years of social shortcomings. I had a job in downtown Atlanta and I could buy my own clothes and shoes. During the 90's it was real popular for guys to get chemicals put into their hair to make their hair curly without the wet moisture of the 80's Jeri curl. So I would get my hair "done" at a shop in Atlanta and with my new look I stepped into Redan High School with a new found bounce in my step. That bounce in my step caught the eye of females that did not know me. I was now the "cute" guy.

Girls….yummy, yum, yum; ninth grade was the best school year of my entire life, including graduate school. I think I must have been God's favorite because he helped me produce the biggest socio/environmental weather pattern change in the history of teenagers. I had a girlfriend that was a senior. Yep, let that simmer a bit. Middle finger to that guy, grab my crouch to those guys, ha, ha, ha, ha. She was ridiculously gorgeous, most of the guys at school liked her but out of the blue this skinny 9th grader was her boyfriend. Cue the song "We are the champions".

Stop laughing, this really happened. Now I think I'm hot stuff, and the other guys are thinking, "Hey, he must be cool if she is with him" and the girls were like "Wow, he must be awesome if he is with her." My reputation could not be better and for a while it was. I still had some lapses on the basketball court that followed me to high school and I could not get away from the fact that my hands dragged on the ground and I could not control my constantly changing body in order to be effective at the sport of basketball. I might have to let that dream go for good. Life was happening and I had to come down from my social high after I was rocked with some disturbing relationship news.

Here we go again

Not too long before prom season I got a card from my super ultra-mega lightning hot girlfriend informing me that she did not want to go to the prom with me. Damn, the social demons got to her. She could not go to her senior prom with a 9th grader because that would have been social suicide. I was devastated; we had to break up because of that. I could not save face. In hindsight, her reasoning is understandable but I was hoping she would have been brave enough to endure the social beating she would have taken in making that decision and that was something that she was not willing to do. I got over it quickly.....like THE NEXT YEAR BABY!!!! Tenth grade was a repeat of the ninth grade and this time I garnered the attention of another upper classman this time she was a junior. That was a good relationship for me.

I learned more life lessons from it and we both benefited from each other's love years later. Throughout these good times my evolution was flowing well but now I needed my father more because the introduction of females into my life created another series of questions that needed answering. My mom was incapable of helping me on these topics and JL's influence was appreciated but diluted due to the complexity of the topics and some things I was afraid to share with him *just because*. Once again, I made another significant deposit of anger and memories into my "little box". I don't remember everything regarding that time of my life. There are some gaps. I think those gaps were sent my way to help me move forward. Later on, towards the end of my school years, various awards ceremonies, basketball games and such, my father was not there. One event he did show up and—wow, this just popped in my head; I remember JL was there along with my mom and he looked uncomfortable with JL's presence.

When they called my name for the award they said "E. Lee Harden II" and I remember he took offense to my shortening the name that he and I both share. Not the response that I was looking for at an awards ceremony and my mom was not pleased at all. Told you, I was trying my best to not be like him. I felt like in shortening my name I would not be associated with being him or being like him.

Later on I decided to go by my middle name Lee as the default and I use that to this day.

By the time I was 18 years old my "little box" had become some sort of incubator of hatred that radiated deep inside my soul. My biologically gifted temper was only tempered by my mother's strong hand. Away from her I was out of control on the insides. There was an emotional hurricane swirling around in my spirit with no outlet, no relief valve, and no pressure release. My anger swelled and grew. The rage was born; it was something that I thought I could manage. The truth is I had no idea what I was in for.

Cancerous Anger

I remember one night while my mom was asleep I cried to myself. This was not your standard cry; this was bone aching, head throbbing, weeping tears of pain. I dared not make too much noise because my mom would have heard me down the hall. I had to be quiet, but it hurt so badly. I was experiencing a crack in my "little box".

Something got out, a thought, a memory, something got out and when combined with a relating experience triggered an outpouring of emotion that I could not stop. My pillow did not stand a chance. Fold it over to the dry side and cry some more, Lee. Pull the sheets over your face so your mom can't hear you. Now you are hot and sweating, your t-shirt is wet from tears and body heat. "Why does he not want me?" was the question I was asking myself. After a couple of hours, exhaustion would set in and I would have to get up and go to school, tired and sad, only to endure more social drama to compound my feelings further into the toilet. Didn't I tell you earlier kids can be A-holes?

This cancerous anger was bad news; it was something I had to monitor. If I got into a fight or lost my temper I knew I might not be able to control myself. Towards my senior year of high school I learned how to ignore the social issues and I was looking forward to the virtual reset button that college could provide me. My anger was stronger than ever and I knew I had to do something about it. I decided to use it to my advantage.

I'll show you

I am feeling anxious writing this, I have not written anything in weeks. It is hard to open up and put down the thoughts that I have regarding all of this. I have a headache right now and I seem to always feel bad after writing for a couple of hours but this is important for me and I hope you can understand how this can be difficult for me. Okay, enough of that, college was interesting for me. My undergraduate experience was good. I went to a school that was well respected for the major that I chose and I was very successful academically. This was surprising to me because I felt that I was not a good student due to the academic challenges of high school. College was different: I was by myself and alone with my thoughts. I enjoyed the social anonymity that it provided me and yet I felt that empty gap in my life again. Maybe I was jealous of other student's parents when they came up to drop them off after breaks and such--I'm not sure. Either way, I developed this desire to prove to my father that I could make it in life without him. I wanted him to see my success and feel bad for not being along for the ride. I know this was not the right way to go about it but at the time I was reaching for something to motivate me to perform. Michael Jordan often used press clips from his opponents to motivate him and he would drop a billion points on that person's team the next night and I figured I could convert my anger into a resource for me to use as fuel for my personal success.

Spiteful? Yes. Did my father deserve it? Yes. But I knew deep down inside that this was not the right way to handle it. Let me tell you something about real emotional pain. This kind of pain is like white water rapids, there may be a calm point prior to them and after them but they are still there and when you are going through them you think, "oh crap, I'm going to die" but when you make it through them you are okay. The problem is with this type of pain, the calm points vary and sometimes you feel like you are riding the rapids all of the time and you have that "oh shit, I'm going to die" feeling everyday.

It comes on so quickly, so intensely I don't know how I managed to keep my sanity. I'm messed up. I bet some physiologist/ Dr. Phil type is reading this and saying, "This dude is messed up". I know. And maybe I need some form of therapy. But this here is my therapy. I feel relieved of the pressure that I have inside and that "little box" does not glow so brightly every time I sit down and put these words down. Can you really blame those individuals who lose their minds and become violent because of their past experiences?

Crazy people do crazy things all of the time, so why am I not as messed up as those guys? Trauma is something that affects people differently, yet I think it is something that we ignore in our society. Don't get me wrong I'm not trying to go into some form of social ethics lesson here but I'm trying to give you some insight into why people react to pain in different ways.

Wonder Woman

Wow, how do I put this into words? Being a mother is difficult. You have this little person that is depending on you for everything and of course, there is no manual that tells you how to do it. Most mothers have a husband, significant other, partner, or somebody to assist them in raising a child or children if you got a two or more. What if you did not have a husband, significant other, partner, or somebody to assist you with raising your child? What do you do then?

In my opinion being a single mother is one of the hardest jobs a person could have. Some people excel at it like my mother does and others may not be as successful. How can you quantify a single mother's success? If that child is a failure does that mean the mother failed too? No, not necessarily; all mothers want the best for their children. It is up to the child to make the correct life decisions based on the primary programming (lessons) from their mothers. If a child is sorry in life that is not the mother's fault, we are all individuals and we make our own decisions.

However, without a strong mother's teachings it is hard to make the right decisions. I guess am lucky in that aspect. I might have not had the best father in life *but what I lacked in a father I had everything that I needed in a mother.* For as long as I can remember, my mother has always been committed to my well-being. I know what you are thinking "aren't all moms committed to their children's well-being?" Yes, but it's different to me and I am going to attempt to frame it for you in a way that you can understand what I am trying to say.

I believe that my mother has always cared for me with an intensity that I have for my own children. She has forgone meals, trips, relationships, and countless other sacrifices just to ensure my well-being. This woman--a manager by trade--was totally dedicated to me. I remember as a little boy we lived somewhere in Columbus Ohio and on Christmas I got a letter from Santa. "Santa" told me he did not have any toys for me for Christmas. At the time we were staying on the first floor of this rather large home with no furniture, I do remember I had a bed. We moved and I remember on another Christmas I got a toy that I really wanted but I thought I was not able to have. I was so happy; my mom always had a way of "making things happen." I can only imagine what she had to sacrifice for me to get that particular toy. I am not trying to say that our situation was bad because it was not in my eyes. Yes, there are kids with more difficult situations but mine was not that bad.

Maybe that is the magic that my mother was able to create in keeping me from knowing the challenges she was facing. This is what makes single mothers special. They have the ability to shield their children from things that could scare them or cause them pain. It makes me sad when I think about single mothers doing all of that without having someone there to help them cope with all of life's challenges. Think about it, these women were still sorting life out when their children came along and they had to endure all of those experiences while keeping a filter from their children and dealing with the fucked up things that life puts in front of them. Then, you have to think about the fact that my mom was raising a boy and she probably knew that I would have some issues with not having my father in my life. She knew that I would be getting bigger and soon she would be dealing with a stupid hormone-fueled teenager with aggression issues, both in temperament and appetite.

Yet, she continued to be a mother to me and I hope I did not cause her too much grief. For so many years it has been just her and me, no one else. I depended on her for everything. The problem was I was getting tall. Very tall, and her 5'6" body would soon be looking up to a 6'6" son that outweighed her by 50 pounds. I assume she had to make a decision, be the type of mother that was soft and squishy and risk my not respecting her or sacrifice the closeness that we had and be a mother and father to me.

This "tough love" approach is bittersweet to me. I understand why she had to be that way because if she did not it would be very hard for her to keep me in check as I was maturing and I get that. What makes me upset is the fact that she had to make that choice. If my parents were together my mom could have been the warm and squishy mother that I wanted. If my father was in my life on a consistent basis maybe she would not have had to make the choices and sacrifices that she did because of his lack of financial assistance. That part upsets me.

Discipline was not a problem for my mom. Our home was set up in a way that gave me limited freedoms but I was allowed to explore my environment and if I was out of line I would quickly be "reminded" to fall in line with a trademark glare from the corner of her eye or well-placed back-handed smack to the mouth if needed. Did I mention that discipline was not a problem for my mom? I had chores just like everyone else and I had responsibilities like everyone else.

One thing that was different about our home was how it operated. During my youth my mother worked crazy hours and sometimes I had to take care of myself at home and alone at an early age. We had a system of phone calls that were made during the day. A call when I got home from school, a call when I should be doing my homework, and if I left home I had to call to tell her where I was going. Oh, and don't let my homework be wrong. She would wake me up and I would have to make the corrections whenever she came home from work. I appreciate all of that now. I understand the reasoning behind all of that.

As a teenager I felt like she was being hard on me but what she was really doing was preparing me. She was preparing me for life, and those tough lessons were needed in order to give me the moral fortitude to deal with all of the shit that life had to offer. Sure there were some things that she just could not help me with because she did not have the "tools". But she did her best at the things that she was equipped for and she used all of her "tools" and borrowed some more "tools" from others to make sure I got what I needed in my early years.

This brings us back to what is a single mother's measure of success? Hmm....I guess I would have to say that a single mother's success is a child who can stand up on his or her own feet, a child that is living in the fashion that the mother has trained them, along with following the moral and social standards that she placed in him or her. As a black man, I guess I'm supposed to be a success just in the fact that I was able to finish high school. Not to mention undergraduate school and graduate school. I learned at an early age that what I do reflects on my mother. Not because she used to say that to me (even though she always told me that) but because my accomplishments are validation for all of the sacrifices that she made. I think a single mother's success is her children's success. We all will have failures but we share our triumphs with our mothers along with our failures.

The trick is to have more triumphs than screw-ups. I am learning now that our lives will always be tied together. Even as a grown 37-year-old man, my mother will always succeed in my accomplishments and now the accomplishments of my children. As a father now I have to pass on the lessons that I learned from my mother. I hope that my mom can be the soft and squishy grandmother that I wanted as a mother. I am excited for her to have the opportunity to see another generation come into the world without the challenges that she had growing up and in raising me. I secretly crave the ability to give her all of the material things that she has never had in life. I would love for her to be able to quit her job and enjoy life without financial worries.

Unfortunately, I am not one of those NBA guys and I cannot do that for my mother…yet. But I am working on it. Until then I am going to do my best in this world that she brought me into. I'm going to continue putting my foot up life's ass by doing the things that I believe will make me a better person. Just as she would want me to, because I desperately want to make her proud of me and I don't want to let her down. She is more than a mother to me; she is my first role model, my tickle buddy, and my own real life super hero, she is my own personal Wonder Woman.

One Way Letter

Dear father,

I hope you are doing well. I am not sure how you will receive this but I hope you have learned how I have developed and matured over the years. I did not write this book to hurt you in any form or fashion. The purpose of this book is to help me heal from the pain that I had (have) from you not being a consistent part of my life. I am hoping that someone reading this book can also heal from it as well. To be honest with you, growing up was very difficult for me without you. I can remember you and mom having conversations about clothes that were bought and other things that I did not understand. I just wanted us to hangout and play. Telling you this as a grown 37-year-old man is kinda embarrassing to me but at the time your presence was all that I wanted.

Like I mentioned in the book, the best times with you that I can recall are the couple of years that I stayed with you and R. You always made me feel comfortable and safe and we had a great time. After my mother took me back to Ohio I did not see you for a while and as I grew older you became more of a mystery to me than a father. Then there was a point were we had a normal relationship and I even had a dog. I really enjoyed that time period. At that point you were a super hero to me. You had muscles and a cool car and I wanted desperately to be just like you. I remember the lessons that you taught me. I remember you letting me sit in your lap and drive your car. I even remember your albums and me listening to you play your harmonica.

Then it happed, you disappeared. For years I lost track of you and I don't know what happened. During that time apart things was terrible. I wrote about that earlier and I don't want to rehash that now but it was bad. I am not blaming you for my failures in sports. Those things were due to my own lack of skills. However, with your support and understanding of how to use our hideous temper (family trait) to my advantage, maybe I could have applied it towards something more positive. Maybe I could have been more competitive instead of the soft-spoken insecure teen that I was. Back then I was so angry. I truly hated you. I am ashamed to say that here but I was hurting so bad. You hurt me so bad. Then we found you and we tried to patch things up again. This time you were married to P. and she had 2 little boys. I hated those damn boys. I hated everything about them. What really hurt me the most was they had the nerve to call you "Daddy". There reverence for you was staggering, I was truly jealous of the fact that they had you 100% of the time and you and I had a relationship that was similar to bread crumbs in substance. I never really wanted anything material from you because I remember you complaining about what you bought when I was younger so I did not want to ask you for anything really. I just wanted you to spend time with me.

I don't know if you are aware of how your decisions have affected me. I am better now but I am still puzzled at your lack of desire to be a part of my life. I was glad that you were very interested to be at my wedding and I was glad you were there and I appreciate you keeping a low profile. That was a great day and I would pay money to know what you were thinking when our eyes met on occasion during that

Lee Harden   49 day. You were smiling ear-to-ear, and I knew you were proud of me. Once again I was hoping for our relationship to be rekindled but it did not happen.

Then my wife and I started our family and that is when everything changed for me. When my oldest son was born I stupidly, thought you would once again, change your tune and maybe relish the opportunity to be a grandfather to my son. This opportunity was not only something that you were not interested in but I felt like your lack of interest in him was a rejection of me and my own child, your own flesh and blood. The anger and forgiveness that I once gave you disappeared. Sadness filled my heart and the anger returned. This time not for me but for my own child. This was further compounded when we had our second son. Twice rejected, and twice ignored.

This has rocked me to my core. I don't know what to think now. All of the steps and systems that I outlined in this book cannot undo the pain of those series of decisions that you made. You turned your back not only to me but you turned your back to your own flesh and blood. I can't wrap my mind around the justification for it. Yes, I am a grown man and the telephone works both ways but now I do not desire to push any buttons relating to contacting you. I can't. I can't put my boys in the same situation that I grew up in. I won't. As a grown man I respect you and what you stand for in my life.

You may not know this but I am a very confident man now. I understand who I am and I understand who we are as a family. Like you all Hardens are hard working. Our talent is not musical like most large families from Dayton Ohio but we are hard working, quick tempered, people with a strong sense of purpose and a stronger sense of survival. From your father Warren G all the way down to the newest Harden infant, that "fight" that we have is a part of our DNA. That is what makes us who we are. This could have been something that I learned from you but I had to learn that on my own. I had to research my own family identity and what I love about your brothers and sister and their children is they are all like me. They talk like me, they look like me, and they all have the "fight" in them like I do. They are all great people even if divided at times, and they love you too.

You might not see it but they are a part of you and you don't even know it. Each one of your siblings has a specific trait that makes you guys different yet the same. You remind me of your big brother so much. That is probably why him and I get along so well. I want you to know that he loves you. He does not like who you are today but he <u>still</u> loves you. I hope that one day you can be closer to him than you are now.

I worry about how things are going to be for you and I in the future. I was sad to see you in pain at your mother's funeral. It was hard for me to be there because I did not know how you were going to receive me. I don't know how things are going to be going forward. Maybe you will see the boys at family events maybe you will be upset with me for writing this book and you might not want to talk to me. Either way things are going to change; I cannot worry about how you may feel going forward. I have to protect what matters to me the most. I have two boys that need me the way that I once needed you. I accept your not wanting to be a part of their lives and for their own good I intend on keeping their lives separate from yours. I will talk to them about our relationship when they are old enough but for now I have to protect them from the disappointments and struggles that you have caused and I'm still dealing with as an adult.

I'm mentally exhausted at this point. I'm searching for words and my desire to write further is fading. I don't know what is going to happen in the future. I hope that when you read this book you learn more about me and I hope that you understand the progress that I have made since I left your home so many years ago. I am a good man, I think if you sat down and talked to me you would be proud of the man and father that I have become.

Right now that is not possible, my anger has returned not with the same intensity as before but now it is more concentrated, more focused, yet sadder. Then it goes away, because I am always thinking about those 2 little souls asleep above me in their beds and I can only think about them. Do you ever think about me?

Love,

Lee Harden

Part II The Transformation

Fragile: Handle with care

Humans are fragile. We think we are indestructible but we are so incredibly fragile and because I was a male I thought I was made of steel, which is why kids are always trying to kill themselves by doing crazy things. One car accident, one bad fall, one bad decision, and your life can either end or be dramatically compromised. The messed up thing about physical damage to our bodies is that it is not the most fragile thing about us. The human mind is more fragile than the body. The mind controls the whole show and if your mind is not right, your body will follow that same path.

That's why I have to get this stuff out of my head; I have to purge my soul of this cancerous anger. I don't want it to manifest into something that could affect my health.

I remember when I was younger I would cry a lot, I would cry all of the time. I don't know why I did-- I just felt weird. There was a sense of fear and uncertainty that I had at a young age and I did not know how to feel when I was living with my father and away from my mother. I did not understand, at the time, why they were not together and all of us living under the same roof like my father's "step-family".

As a father of two boys now, I am very aware of their feelings and I try to provide them a sense of safety, consistency, and love that I felt I did not have when I was their age. This is the charge that I guess all parents have. We are responsible for our children in every kind of way. We have to provide them with the basics, of course, but we also have to ensure that they are happy and we have to teach them how to essentially manage their emotions. It's a tough job indeed but because of my understanding of what I needed as a child I am more conscious of their mental health and I hope that they will never need their own "little box".

I want their perception of me to be everything that I did not see in my own father. What does that mean? Well, it could be made up of several things but I would summate them in these categories: *presence, consistency, demonstrating, support,* and *affection.* These are the 4 behaviors that I think children need from their fathers in their homes. I cannot speak for girls or mothers because I don't know. I am an expert however on what *I* needed as a child. Maybe this could help you understand me or maybe you feel the same way.

Presence

In my humble opinion a man's presence in a home is very important. During the short time that I stayed with my father, just seeing him on a daily basis was great. The relational dynamics of the entire household with step-wife and step-daughter + me (biological child) was the weird part. Like I said earlier--seeing a man that I could look up to and pattern myself after, aspire to be like, and observe was everything. Fast forward to my early teen years, given a man's consistent daily presence I may have had a better time trying to press the copy button and create my own male identity. I would not be totally original because the man I would be getting my "clues" from would not be my biological father but the execution would have been better than me doing it by myself. This of course is no fault of my mother, it's just something that could not have been corrected without someone romantically in her life and like I said earlier *she did not play that, you had to be on your game to get remotely near me.* A man's presence in a home is also important in basic learning. Simple "guy" stuff like fixing the kitchen sink or changing the vacuum bag are things that I find my oldest son watching with great intensity and curiosity. I'll get into that more in a moment but I don't want to give you the impression that if you are a single mother of a boy you MUST have a man in the home.

My message to single mothers is *you MUST have a prototype.*

This person does not have to be a romantic interest, he does not have to be someone that feels obligated to be a "father figure," he just has to have an interest in your boy and they have to get along. Given the amount of time spent and the nature of their friendship the boy will "press copy" when the time is right. Here is where your "Mom Powers" have to be on point. The person that you put in front of your boy has to be of merit and *worthy of being replicated.* This is very, very, important. A bad person with bad behavior and bad intentions is not the person you want your boy trying to emulate. This is can backfire severely. You want this man to represent what you feel is a good man with the morals and the character that you believe are good.

Consistency

No one likes an indecisive man and to a child, a man that has a word that is worth something is very important. You have seen it on television before, the kid sitting in front of the front door waiting for Daddy to come. Let me tell you that sucks, big time, I was that kid. My father's word was worthless to me. His lack of consistency in following through on the things that he promised made me not trust him and to this day I have problems getting excited about things.

Here is the clue for all parents; if you can't make it happen then tell your children the truth. "Little Ray-Ray, Little Chandler, Little Becky, Mommy can't do that." This is a hell of a lot better than saying "yes" and then you have to eat those words later. As a father now I made a promise to myself that my word to my boys will be concrete. A "yes" means hell yeah it is going to happen. A "maybe" means it's possible but we will have to see what happens. A "no" means don't freaking ask again. Three simple options that is both definitive and direct. I think this is a no-brainer for most parents but from a father this is almost on par with the *10 Commandments.*

Demonstrating

This is one of the most important facets of the relationship that I needed from my father. The demonstrating portion of a father's presence is essential because this is your direct opportunity for a boy (remember I cannot speak on girls) to learn behavioral idiosyncrasies of their father. Simple activities like how he shaves, how he holds his cup, stupid little things that you may take for granted are totally being watched and recorded by young boys. They want to move, walk, act, stand, eat, urinate, everything like Daddy. The way they learn is through observation and without that resource it only makes things more difficult. This process of demonstrating along with being consistent in performing this act is critical to boy's confidence and their understanding of who they are along with bonding with their fathers or father figures.

Support

This is probably one of the biggest and most enduring aspects of the father/son relationship that I needed and that other kids like me needed. My "finishing father" JL is very, very good at this. He has always been a constant resource and soundboard for my stupid questions, stupid ideas, stupid desires, stupid dreams, stupid relationships, stupid life theories, and general idiotic sub-teenage life learning lessons. Never once, did he shoot down my ideas, never told me it could not be done. He has never said something that I wanted to do was not possible.

His honesty in teaching me how to navigate through life is very dear to me. He is my Encyclopedia Britannica with a beard. Always positive, always very loving, as a kid I gave him the title of "Papa Bear" which is code for the non-biological relationship that we have. Single mothers, this is the prototype that I spoke of earlier. This man is the type of person that you want your young boy to "press copy" from. I guess I was lucky. The beauty of the support from a man that is different from mothers is it comes without all of the fluff. Men don't really respond to things in the way that women do and while I love my mom, JL's viewpoint on things can skew from being the same to freakin' totally nowhere near the same at all. During those terrible teen years, JL's support was invaluable in my early relationships and those lessons learned carried me through undergrad in college. I cannot imagine how I would have made it without him.

Our relationship is the greatest gift my mother ever gave me. Like I said--*he was on his game when he was dating my mother.* Unfortunately, he never married my mother. On the plane ride back from my undergraduate graduation he surprised both of us with an invitation to his upcoming wedding. "Oh s!@#", I thought. I almost instantly got that familiar feeling in my soul that I was about to be abandoned again. Huh, you say? Yes, I was 22 years old and I was scared to death that our relationship was going to change. Or worse yet, we would not be able to maintain the same type of relationship. Would I be able to call him when I had a question about something? Could we have our occasional moments alone to shoot the breeze and I bounce ideas off of him about what I wanted to accomplish in life? Would all of the things that we have shared over the years become different now that he is marrying someone other than my mother? I had a huge rock in my stomach, I thought "Oh well, it was nice while it lasted". I was reassured when he told me that he spoke with his wife BW, and he told her that I was a "package deal". Meaning, I was not something that he would just drop like a hot bowl of grits. Reassured, I went to his wedding and had a blast. BW has always treated me with the love and tenderness of a biological mother, both of them adding muscle and skin to the skeleton of a boy that needed finishing.

Affection

I don't know how to address this without sounding weird. The last thing that I feel was missing was my father's affection. A pat on the head is one thing but I would equate it to more than that. Hugs, a handshake, a kiss on the forehead, are things that I wanted at home. My father was very good at this for the year or so that I stayed with him. As a father now I try to show my boys my affection for them in different ways. I kiss them, I play with their ears and tickle them to the point they fart with laughter. I enjoy roughhousing with them, playfully smacking the older one in the back in order to toughen him up. Wrestling with both of them on Saturday mornings is another thing that we enjoy as a family. This is something that my mom and I used to do when I was little but it is very different when it's just the boys and me.

It reminds me of the stuff that you see on National Geographic where the little cubs may be playing but the skills that they are practicing in play will be used later on in real life. Is the absence of affection from my father at home more significant than the other four categories? Yes, because it blends in with a mother's love and gives you a sense of warmth and love that makes a family a family. The other four are interdependent. Affection is the only one, in my opinion, that can stand alone on its own. I'd take affection over all of the rest if I had to choose one. It's the demonstration of the emotion of love. Every child can pick up on that, it's the foundation of a lifelong relationship and without it you can be whole and empty at the same time.

So that is the whole picture of what I feel was needed from my father in a mashed up kind of way. I'm not trying to minimize what you might think is needed; this is based on my experience and yours could be different of course. This is my impression of what could have made things better for me but I would like to take that further and talk to you about what it would be like if both parents where home.

Two Piece

There are few people that I hate in the world but one type of person that really rubs me the wrong way is the *complaining kid with both parents at home*. I would not say I hate this person but if you could buy a ticket to slap someone as strong as you can, this would be the person I would spend a good $200 bucks on. These people have no concept of what it is like to live in a single parent household. They don't know how financially better off they are because of their parents being together. They say stupid crap like "my Dad got me a Honda but I wanted a Mercedes." Oh shut the hell up, with their mothers making their breakfast for them everyday before school. Really, seriously, I knew someone that had a mother that did not work and she made his breakfast everyday and he was dropped off at school. This was unheard of in my circle of friends. But his situation is probably the life that all of us really wanted and I was just hating on him because I did not have that. I don't care. Yeah, I was jealous and when I was younger I wanted my parents to be together so bad. I never really thought about how my parents would get along if they did not divorce and I guess I should have. Does that make me selfish for wanting my parents to be together even though they would not be happy? Would I rather them be unhappy and have that experience growing up? What would you rather deal with? Hmmm...let me think.

Growing up in a situation that has elements of violence and/or unhappiness I'm sure would be another book but would I trade that for my experience? No, I would not, I'm sure that there are some people out there that have lived in homes that were not always peaceful and just because a man is present at home does not mean he is happy in that home.

To choose a life with a father in the house at the expense of my mother's happiness and safety would be selfish on my part. Look at some other forms of home structure; Mom or Dad that works all of the time, this household makes a ton of money but their kids will be drug addicts because they did not see their parents and felt ignored. What about the cheating parent? Mom and Dad argue all of the time and Dad goes away all of the time "for work." Then they get divorced and now your step-mother is six years older than you. Wow. Then there is the abusive father. This is tough because everyone in the home has to deal with Dad and his temper issues. The wife withdraws and tries to protect the children. The daughter is afraid of her dad and may turn to the wrong people for love. The son does not know how to deal with authority and lashes out at school. This is probably the worst type of situation that could occur when both parents are at home.

The funny thing about all of this is these are actual examples of homes in our country. Once again, I could have had any of these types of situations in my life and when you think about what could have happened I have greater perspective of what my life experience has been to this point. Doesn't mean it did not suck in some aspects but it is not as bad as some other person's life, easily.

I don't want to give you the impression that my life was bad because it was not--there are plenty of good and great points. Growing up to this point in this book has been hard but now that I had found out who I am and how I see myself I still had to deal with the elephant in the room. How do I deal with the pain? How do I change the anger into something that will not erode my soul? I can't focus on other people's life experiences and I respect what others may have gone through, but now--as a young man--I had to figure out how to manage being me.

Coming out of college I was feeling pretty good about myself. I landed a decent job and bought my first home. My confidence was pretty good, I had a cute girlfriend from college and a little money in my pocket but I pushed my emotions and feelings to the back burner. To be honest, that was one of the greatest mistakes that I ever made.

You see, I learned so because after that I had to deal with some demons inside me and I made my first critical mistake. I was working quite a bit and my girlfriend at the time was living with my roommate and me. She was getting ready for work and we were arguing. It was over a movie and that was totally stupid but during the fight she went into the bathroom and slammed the door in my face. All of a sudden a sense of rage came over me and I thought "She can't close the door in my face. This is MY home," and I shoved the door open with my shoulder. In doing so the door swung open wildly and hit her in the hip.

My girlfriend cried in pain from both the impact of the door and the violent nature of my action. It was not too long after that when we broke up. A relationship cannot survive with stuff like that going on. I apologized to her like crazy and I felt like some abusive husband begging for forgiveness. If she is reading this I would like to apologize again for hurting her in both ways. I'm not trying to make excuses for my actions but this was a wake-up call for me that I had to deal with this "little box" or I could get into some major trouble.

Maybe I was becoming the guy that could not control himself because of his past? I'm not sure. What I do know is that experience was very sad; I lost one of the best relationships that I had ever had. I threw it away. Of course I am very thankful for my wife and my children but I never wanted to loose someone because of that. That is not the man that I am today and that one time I lost my temper and I lost someone that was very important to me. I have never lost my temper since then. I have been very conscious of my emotions since then and after that I was by myself for a couple of years. During the years of 2000-2005 I got into my career and had several relationships and I rarely dealt with the pain that I was carrying. I was ignoring my feelings at the time and I was just going through life on autopilot.

I assume most people have done this and maybe they are more successful at either hiding their pain or potentially forgetting it. No matter how hard I tried I was not good at ignoring what was going on inside of me. I knew that I had to let the pain go. I did not know how to do it. I was scared about confronting it. I knew that I had to figure out a way to deal with the pain and I will explain how I got through it and then I will tell you about the night that I freed myself of it.

How to manage your pain

Okay, here are the meat and potatoes of what you can do to get through the pain and this may help you:

1. Know that the pain is real; it's not imaginary. There are no fake feelings that come and go. These thoughts that you have are just manifestations of your feelings and they are real and if you don't deal with them they <u>will</u> deal with you.

2. You are not the reason your mother or father did not want to be in your life. You can't blame yourself for a decision that they made. I know that our first thought is to blame ourselves but we cannot make someone do something that they do not want to do. Knowing this, we are not responsible for their actions. This is very important.

3. History cannot be changed; as much as you want things to be different you cannot continue to look back. Further, you cannot expect someone to change their behavior after they have been consistently behaving the same way for years. If your mother or father is still living and has not changed their relationship with you then don't expect it to happen. This is something I am going through right now as I AM TYPING THIS SENTENCE. You will drive yourself crazy trying to understand why they don't want to change. So don't expect them to change. If they are still living and they don't want to be bothered with you then don't be bothered with them.

4. If they do want to be in your life then you have to make that decision to either allow them to be in your life and the extent of their involvement in your life or you can just leave them alone. Either way the choice is yours. *Don't give people the power to control your feelings.*

5. Take ownership of the situation. What I mean by that is: you have to get in front of the issue. By dealing with your feelings you are taking control of them instead of being behind the issue by not addressing your feelings. This can be accomplished by getting professional help or maybe writing about it like me. Either way, you have to grab a hold of the thing that is hurting you the most and choke it. Imagine you are falling in the sky and your pain is a stranger that is on top of you. Even though both of you are falling towards the earth, the pain in the form of a stranger is trying to push you under it so your back is towards the ground. What I am saying is, take control of the situation and grab that pain by the throat and get on top of it. So now you are the one on top and your pain is the stranger with their back towards the ground. Hell, if we are going to hit the ground you are going to hit it first, buddy.

6. Uncork the bottle and let it out. This is the hardest part of the process. You will feel better afterwards but it is something that you must do. You have to open yourself up and deal with your hurt. This is a bitch to go through but you must. You have to let it out, let your pain leave you. Don't hold it back, all of the anger, all of the pain must be out of you. Your soul cannot grow with that hurt in you. Your actions are based on that hurt. Decisions are based on that hurt.

7. The purge is necessary; the problem is most people don't want to purge themselves of the pain. They fear the pain that it would take in order to do it. My point to you is if you don't then you will never heal. Hell, I'm still not healed after I completed this. But I can honestly tell you that after experiencing it I am better in doing so. You are not a coward for holding it in but true bravery is stepping up and looking within and confronting your personal demons.

8. What happens now that you dealt with the pain? Well, you will feel better at first. You may even experience some emptiness now that you have dealt with your pain. This is your opportunity to heal. This is where I am right now AS I AM TYPING THIS SENTENCE. You are putting topsoil back into the crater that your pain was taking up in your heart. This is going to take some time, it is not going to happen overnight but you will be better for it. This is important for you and your family. I hope that writing this can help me get over my pain. This is not just a patch; this is a permanent process that we have to go through for the rest of our lives.

I can't tell you how things will play out for you; I hope that this will help you deal with your pain. This is a summation of what I had to do to deal with my pain but the actual event that drove me to deal with my pain was nothing like the six step process. It was ugly and I will tell you exactly what happened to me and how I got through it.

The Purge

In 2006 I thought I was hot stuff. I left my first home with some new renters from Hurricane Katrina and moved downtown. I wanted to start a new "adult" life in a new place. I was 30 years old and I had a new sports car and a cool loft apartment. I was truly living a bachelor's life; did I mention that I thought I was hot shit? However, one night in my fresh new downtown apartment I had to deal with my pain and that was the hardest night of my life. I don't know what triggered my thoughts; I remember I was lying in my bed again trying to go to sleep when I had this overwhelming feeling of sadness.

This time I did not try to pacify it, I gave up, I allowed it to flow freely. I thought about all of the year's worth of pain and sadness, I thought about all of the days and nights that I cried myself to sleep because I thought my own father did not want me. I thought about the days at the gym not being able to dunk a basketball because my confidence was not there, I thought about all of the broken promises and special events he missed. I thought about all of those things that night and all of the pain that I had been carrying for 30 years rushed out of my soul and ripped me apart from the insides out. This time I could not silence my tears. No need to suppress them now, the place was empty. Just me in the loft alone, this time I did not have the ability to contain my feelings now, too late. Too much emotion flowing, too many tears, maybe it was God's design to have me in such a place. The concrete floors and walls were a perfect barrier for my weeping cries to be contained from my neighbors. I could hear my sobbing reflect back to me from the wall of glass that covered the back of my loft. My screaming echoing back to me in what I felt was stereo sound. I was literally *inside* my "little box" incased in a square room of metal, concrete, and glass. This time my tears flowed violently, I thought "why does he not love me?"

Years of sadness rang out of my lungs and the pain flowed viciously out of my body. I ached physically. I was sick of hurting on the inside and now I was sick of hurting outside. I prayed to God that I would not let it beat me. I sat up in the bed and reached up to the sky and professed to the Lord that I would forgive my father. I told God I did not want this pain anymore and I screamed "'you can have it!" I don't want it anymore!" Then it was over, the pain I felt went away. My body stopped hurting, and my spirit was calming. Once again my sheets were soaking wet with tears and sweat.

My body was sore from the tension in my muscles and I was exhausted. I purged myself of the pain. I was free. The Godly part of all of this was, my fresh loft was destined to be the perfect place for that exact event to occur. It all happened when it was supposed to—as if it was set up to occur from the start. That night I slept well feeling a lot lighter and more reassured about who I was and the male identity that I was searching for was finished in a metal, concrete, and glass box. The copy was complete, and I was whole. I was a man, fully grown, 100% confident in who I was and that was the greatest night of my life as an individual.

Something I heard on the radio

This morning while making my coffee before leaving to work, I heard something that got my attention. The host of the radio show is a well-known game and talk show host and someone that I greatly respect. During the introduction of his radio show he said "if your parents were not the best, don't stress on it, you have to move on". Hmmm....well yeah, that is true but his statement made me think a bit on what I was doing. Was I focusing on the wrong thing? Am I knee deep in the "whoa is me" mentality? Not really, at least I don't think so. Everything I did in life was to show my father that I could make it without him. I used it as a motivational tool.

As I mentioned earlier, the process of using hate and anger to fuel my ambitions may not have been the best practice but *it worked for me*. I get the lesson the radio host was trying to teach his listeners, no one likes a "pity party". I get that; but it's hard to judge someone else's pain. Everyone deals with their pain differently and I think it would be disrespectful to believe that some people should just move on. That is why I raised one eyebrow this morning when I was making my coffee. So could I do a better job at helping someone that is focusing too much on his or her pain? I think so, let's give it a try.

How Do You Get Rid of Your Long-Term Mental Pain?

1. **Own your part of it.** *Everything else, you have to let it go.*

2. **Don't link your pain to your failures.** *Your decisions are your own. The person or persons that hurt you are not responsible for your current situation.*

3. **Looking backwards will not only ensure you hit something but it will also prevent you from moving forward in life.** *You can look back from time to time and it is totally okay to do that. But you have to keep moving forward in life. If you don't, you will never truly heal.*

4. **Break the cycle. If this is a situation that has been a consistent part of your family history or community, do something to ensure that it does not happen again.** *Make the right life choices to eliminate the possibility of that event occurring again.*

5. **Find your release.** *You must find a way to get the pain out. Scream, cry, paint, write a book (yeah, I know), whatever you have to do to get yourself away from the situation that is hurting you. If you don't you might as well be running with a parachute on your back because you are going nowhere.*

Well, I think that sums up what he was trying to say on the radio. I think the difference in what he was saying and what I am saying is, he would like for you to get over your issues and move forward. I am saying that is harder than he may understand and it might take some time to work up to that point. The radio host says instead of being fixated on your situation, you should understand that there

Lee Harden   81 are people in worse situations. Yeah, I get that but who cares? They are not you, I'm sure there are other kids that had terrible childhoods but theirs were not mine. Sorry, I don't give a damn. My reality is just that; *mine*. Here's the bottom line. The best way to defeat your pain is *to succeed in living your life after your painful situation occurred.* This is the best way to give the middle finger to the person or persons who hurt you, the people who said you could not make it, or anything like that. *Your success in how you live your life and the person you are today is the #1 way to beat the pain.*

Fast Forward

That brings us now to today, how do I feel now? I feel pretty good. As I mentioned earlier, I have two young boys that I love with everything I have and they have brought some significant meaning to my life. Five years after I finally figured myself out and became comfortable with the man that I am, I became a father myself and it was glorious. Now it's on me to provide these little persons with the paternal relationship that I always wanted. Is it irony that I have two boys? Don't know for sure. What I do know is when I looked into their eyes not too long after they were born I promised them that I would never leave them. I felt such a sense of love in their eyes when I first saw them. I immediately felt a sense of responsibility to ensure that my experience was not repeated as well. I am trying to paint you a picture of what thoughts go through your mind at that moment.

Unfortunately, you have to be a parent in order to grasp the initial wave of love that you feel for your little people in that clear plastic cart at the hospital. I remember after my first-born's initial bath we were waiting for some tests to come back before going back downstairs to reunite with my wife and I was just sitting there staring at him. He was beautiful, half sleeping in a swaddle that I could not replicate (dammit), with that textbook hospital blue baby hat and white and blue stripped blankets. His gaze at me was piercing, no expectations and no visible sign of emotion. Just mutual curiosity between a child newly born and a father newly made. Maybe he is learning that he has to trust me, maybe that is what is going on during those initial moments of life. Maybe he was thinking "Okay, this guy looks like he cares about me or something, I'm looking at him and he is starring at me." Either way, I knew at that point that this was going to be a life-long relationship that I had to nurture in a way that I felt I needed. The problem is--and I am very aware of it--my over-protective nature regarding my boys. It is something that I am working on.

All of the things that I have told you so far I feel were in preparation for this moment. For me to be a Father, now I have to teach someone things that I may have not been taught. Hell, I don't mind winging it sometimes. I will tell you that it is the scariest thing in the world to go through. You are nervous all of the time for their safety and since they are very young I am constantly trying to keep them from killing themselves or each other or causing the cat to smack them in the face. They are great brothers. I hope that when they are old enough to read this they understand that when it is their turn to be men and then fathers they don't repeat the mistakes that their grandfather made. He has not met them yet and I will discuss that in a moment but I want them to know right here that their grandfather is a good man. Yes, he has made some major mistakes with me and our relationship will probably never be like the one that they have with me. However, if they choose to seek him out I will help them learn as much as they can about him because a small part of the process of them pressing the copy button from me is getting the ink from him.

I love being a husband and a father. Life does not give you instructions on either job and you will probably suck at both at first. Don't kid yourself, I thought it was so simple to go from dating to being married: it's not. Someone should have smacked me if I said that out loud. Now that I have my own family I sit back and I think about my father and sometimes I trip on why he did not want any of this. I understand that he and my mother did not work out but how could you turn your back away from this wonderful feeling of being a dad? Yes, my pain is gone but now I have new questions because I was not a father before. But now I am and the amount of joy that I have in my heart makes me wonder how someone could walk away from it.

Does it hurt? No, not in the sense of the way it affected me when I was younger. I'm 37 now and I'm comfortable in accepting the way my life is right now. However, I do have questions that I don't know if I will ever have the answers for. I've often told my wife that *there is no human on earth that could keep me away from my boys.*

I don't know if you can understand the seriousness of that statement but just understand I will use all 250lbs of my 6 foot, 6 inch frame and someone would be severely hurt or God forbid kill if my boys were in danger. The messed up part about that statement is: I don't think my father felt the same way about me. If he did he wouldn't have let disagreements with my mom keep him away from me, he would have sought me out during my teen years, and he would have had a front row seat at my graduation from college. He does not have that desire to be with me like I have with his grandchildren. That is a shame, because they are great boys. My oldest has several of his features: his love of music, his velvety chocolate brown skin, and the shape of his head. They have not met my father yet and I don't know if they ever will. I am not sure if my father is willing to be a consistent factor in their lives. Their happiness is paramount to me and I will not allow any opportunity for my experiences to be repeated in another

Lee Harden

generation. If asked I would consider it, but I must admit I would be very concerned in doing so. That is where I am right now with things. Come on, judge me as you will. I don't care. I'm sure that some of my family members may read this and be potentially surprised at all of the things that I have revealed here. I'm not sure if they will understand my point of view on this issue and that concerns me. But I can't worry about that, they have their own issues with their parents in various forms and my issues can be viewed in different ways.

I hope that they would see this book as a clue into the character of a cousin that they did not grow up with or the nephew that they did not know that well. Many of them are parents themselves and maybe they share some of the feelings, fears, and concerns that I have about being a parent. As a family, we have a history of division and I'm not going to get too deep in that but I will say this. For the branch of the family tree that I am responsible for, I will not allow my family to fail. I want my family to be close. I know that kids fight and such but I want my kids to be close to each other and it is important to me that they see the love between my wife and me. I hope that I can give them the home life that I was so envious of when I was younger. No, I don't mean spoiling them but I do want them to have experiences that I did not have. As a man-- and keep in mind I am only speaking for myself--I have a strong sense of responsibility for ensuring my family's success. My wife's mother, my mother, our children. JL and his family are all of the people that I think about when I think of my immediate family. I don't want to fail any of them and that fear of failure sometimes is my nemesis.

But I can't worry about that. I don't have the time. The priority right now is taking care of home and that is the only thing that matters to me. Listen, I don't want to come off so cold but after going through all of this who wants to live thinking like that? Screw that. Now I have the opportunity to replace what was lost in my soul by filling in those gaps with my own family experiences and that is what truly makes me happy.

Paying It Forward

This is for the young boys who may be reading this. Maybe your mother gave you this book, or maybe your grandmother or uncle gave this to you. My message to you is very simple. You will not always feel the way you are feeling now. Things will be better, I know you don't think the people closest to you can understand what you are feeling and you are right; they don't. School may not be the best place for you right now but things will get better. Don't let your feelings affect how you act in class because that is not truly who you are. You might be letting your feelings control your actions and not only will that get you in trouble but you are not being a man and taking control of your own situation. By reacting to your feelings negatively you are allowing the people or feelings that are bothering

you to win. Being a man is not just about being "macho".
Being a man is learning how to remain in control of
yourself despite the circumstances that you may be facing.

This is something that you have to practice. You
learned earlier how to deal with the pain but now you have
to take those lessons and really think about how you are
going to live your life day-to-day with the pain. You might
have to take small steps and talk to someone, or get in the
gym and lift some weights to get your mind clear. Remain
nice to people around you especially teachers. If you are
not having a good day at school be honest and if you are
asked, then tell your teacher that you are not having a good
day and just do your work and go home. School is hard
enough and while you are processing your emotions you
don't need extra things going on that will just make you
feel worse. Mr. Teenager, know that we are not the only
ones going through this. There are plenty of young girls,

older people, and young men like you that are going through or went through the same situation that we have.

One of the things that I wish my father would have told me was "I can do anything I set my mind to." I'm here to tell you that you -- Mr. Teenager, Ms. Teenager, or Mr./Mrs. Older Person -- can do anything that you set your mind to. Never let your mind keep you from thinking you can't do something you know you can. For example, during my high school years I was obsessed with dunking like most tall teens.

I was very tall, well over 6'3 and I could jump out of the gym but for some reason I could not dunk a basketball. For some reason I could not will myself enough to jump the additional 5 inches to dunk the ball and it was so disappointing to me. I was laughed at, embarrassed, and miserable for most of my high school years. 10 feet, the rim is just 10 feet off the ground what the heck was going on with me? I'll tell you, my confidence was shot. I did not believe in myself and that was evident in my abilities on the court. Did I really give basketball my best? Maybe not but I know if I had that support that I was craving from my father I would have been better on the court. One normal damn day after school a couple of my buddies and I were on the court and one of them asked me very casually "can you dunk?" and he bounce-passed me the ball and I took a step and jumped straight up with two feet and dunked the ball. It was effortless; it was so easy I could not believe I was not dunking more all of the years before. It was one of the best days of my life because it happened in front of all of the guys that used to give me a hard time. I felt great, vindicated, and accepted something that I secretly wanted so badly.

After I had some time to think about it, I noticed that my self-confidence was keeping me on the ground. All of those years I could have been yoking on guys but I did not believe in myself. That's when I got angry. But you don't have to be angry, Mr. Teenager, because you are reading this and you now understand how your head can take you out of the game in literal and figurative ways. Believing in yourself is something that you have to do for yourself. Don't let what someone says or has done to you make you believe you are less than "<" who you are. Take that pain and apply it to everything that you do.

Be the Kobe Bryant of your life. Develop a "killer instinct" and work to be the best at anything you decide on doing. Let your success show the "haters" how you handle your business. Oh, and while we are on the subject of haters, they will never go away. Take it from a 37-year-old ex-teenager. *The haters just get older and more cowardly as you age.* Knowing this, you can't put too much energy into what they say. Yeah, this sounds corny but it's true; they are going to say whatever but in the end you will go your way and they will go on to do whatever after your senior year. Until then, just continue doing you and the haters will either fall in line or get dealt with (you know what that means).

This is a very important time of your life and college will be a lot better, I promise. Right now get your grades together and learn as much as you can. Life will only get better for you; right now you have to work on yourself and enjoy the people who are supporting you.

Mothers, you may find this stuff hard to figure out; teens are weird by nature and you are not supposed to understand them all of the time. However, on that rare occasion where he/she opens up to you this is your chance to shut up and listen to what they have to say. I cannot speak for girls but for young boys it is a weird time in their life because they want to be open with you moms but they are trying to be independent while going through a period in life in which they are missing a father figure. Make it very comfortable for them to come to you with their concerns, if you fail to do this you could potentially loose the opportunity for a straight line of communication with your teen that could make a significant difference in their personal and academic lives. Refrain from talking negatively about the absentee family member, this does not help the teen's feelings it may even backfire and make the teen desire that person's presence more and if that teen is let down it could be very bad for him/her emotionally. I think my mom did a good job of shielding me from most of the things that were going on in my parent's failed marriage. I know that my reverence for my father when I was young may have been painful but she never "popped my bubble" when it came to my father.

Once I grew up and saw how things played out with my own eyes I saw what she was talking about. The broken promises, the missed events, blah, blah. Moms, I wish I could tell you something in this book to prevent your teen from having the same amount of rage and negative emotions that I had. But I can't guarantee it.

Your teen may have a harder time than I did; your teen may lash out negatively in school and totally withdraw from you and other family members. The best thing you can do for your teen is love them and pay attention to them. If they talk to you, listen to them without critique or questions unless solicited. If you think you need to bring in additional support for your teen then do it; a professional may be better equipped to handle your teen than you are. Maybe I should have seen someone in the past but the main idea is to get resources and lines of communication in place to ensure that your teen has the best chances of getting through this tough period of life.

Moms and Dads, have you ever dealt with the pain that you may have forgotten about regarding your own parents? Have you forgotten what your childhood was like? Maybe you had parents who died early in your life? Have you dealt with your pain? Have you forgiven family members that may have taken advantage of you? We all have people that are close to us that may have hurt us deeply. One certainty that I do know is they will never have any impact in your life ever again and whatever they became in their life is nothing compared to you. If you believe in something greater than you then you understand that people don't succeed when they hurt people like that. Their imprint on you may be minute but the memories of the pain that they may have inflicted on you changed who you are. Knowing this, you cannot allow your children to experience that type of pain alone. You have to share your experiences with your teenage daughters and sons. You have to explain to them how you felt when you were their age and what you did to get through that difficult time in your life. This builds trust with your teen and that will make your teen more willing to share with you the things that are bothering them.

Your situation is like I said earlier, *yours*. But now you have the chance to help someone get through the pain of a traumatic event or the pain of not having a significant person albeit parent, uncle, or grandparent in their lives. Years or even decades could go by and you may not have dealt with your own feelings regarding a loved one that hurt you. Why not resolve that pain? Why let it show up again in your children? End the cycle and deal with it. Your healing will come from you going through the process of getting it out of your "little box".

What about me? Hmm..to be honest, during the course of writing to you I have learned more about myself. I think I am at a place now that I can let all of this negative stuff go. I look at my own children and I hope that they grow up with me as a consistent positive part of their lives. My oldest son is the same age now as I was when my parents divorced. I have no recall of them being together and that is understandable because my son will probably forget what just happened tonight.

I often reflect on my feelings when I was a little boy. I ponder on how I can make sure that those things that I so desperately wanted from my father are given to my children from me. I feel bad that my father has not met them before. This is my latest dose of pain. When our boys were born I secretly hoped that it would spark something in my father and give him a renewed desire to have a relationship with me and my boys. It did not work. My feelings are hurt once again. This time: no anger, no failed expectations, just a sense of absolute reality. *I can't change him.* I can't make someone do something they don't want to do. Further, I can't put my children in a situation that would be bad for them. So I decided to honor his desire to not be a part of his life and I am choosing to withdraw the notion that he will ever be able to see them. I'd rather he be a part of my past than be a negative part of our children's present.

This is tough to think about. I'm sure I'm going to start a beef (rift) with my family in doing this. People will probably take sides but ultimately I have to do what is right for my family. I have to end the cycle. My love for my children supersedes my personal desire for my father's involvement in my life. I saw him at his mother's funeral in 2012 and I saw pain in his face for the first time in my life. I wonder if he has that kind of pain for me? I wonder if he thinks about me on my birthday? I wonder if he thinks about me when his stepchildren call him dad? I wonder if he thinks about me when someone says they saw a cute picture of my boys on Facebook?

Who knows? Is this something that I will try to suppress in my "little box"? No, it does not hurt anymore. It is more like sadness now. I feel empty, not even willing to give the situation any more energy than it takes to key it here on this computer. I'm numb to it all. I hope my family can understand all of this. I hope that if they chose to read this they would not only learn more about me but more about him too. Maybe it would answer some questions yet to be asked, or maybe too afraid to ask. Their opinion of me is important because I love them all.

However, I love our boys more. Lately, I've noticed that life goes by quickly. More quickly then I think people realize. I feel like I was that little boy living with my father in Kindergarten just a few years ago. I find joy in the things my children like; no, this is not some sub Michael Jackson lost childhood thing, but it is nice to be able to recall and enjoy the good things about being young and playing with your Daddy.

In my home I try to present myself in a manner that I hope the boys would be when they are grown: strong, intelligent, very confident, resilient, loving, and honest. If they have the majority of these characteristics I think I did my job. If they don't succeed in life then I would believe that I failed them. I pray that I am wrong. I know their decisions are their own but I hope I can give them enough wisdom to make the correct ones. Only God knows what the future holds. Morbid, I know, but it's the truth.

Life is a series of choices and just as I am choosing to write to you and tell you everything about me, I have to deal with the choices another person has made. There is a phrase out there that says: "Just because you have an emergency that does not mean it is mine too." Often times we give people power over us. We allow complete strangers to dictate what we do in terms of how we look, talk, and dress. Is it possible that true freedom is doing your best to live your life to your own satisfaction? You have heard of a "tailor made suit" right?

What about having a "tailor made" life? What I am getting at is a drastic change in the way you perceive your life. Less focusing on what you don't have and more focusing on what you do have and what is on the horizon. If you see what you have control of and have the ability to appreciate it, things will not seem as bad. Maybe you don't live in a six bedroom home but your apartment is brand new.

Maybe you don't have a Porsche but your Honda is fun to drive. By looking at what you have already instead of focusing on what you don't, your life can be custom tailored to how you see it. I sometimes have to do this as well. My ambition to succeed sometimes clouds my vision and I don't always see the blessings that I already have. This will prevent you from moving forward because if you can't appreciate what you already have then you will not be given more. Not preaching, just food for thought.

My Turn

The other day my oldest son put one on me. He was playing with some rubber "duckies" during his bath and this particular yellow duck came with three smaller little ducks that sit on the back of the bigger duck, and he said the bigger duck was me. This statement was profound to me because in that moment my 3-year-old son was able to recognize my role as his father and leader of our family. I can't tell you how happy that made me feel.

My little boy understood what my role was for him, his brother, and his Mommy. My heart was beaming, not just because of what he said but the symbolism of what the toy ducks and his comments represented. We have been talking about my story for a while now so I'm sure you can appreciate how that meant so much to me and now that I am a father myself things seem to be better for me. I'm not sad anymore, I'm happy. My children bring me a sense of joy that I can't really explain...but I will try.

Children, you know how they say you will always love your children unconditionally? It's very true: the amount of love that you have for your child is something that in my opinion is the one of the most powerful emotions that God gives us. This strong desire to protect and nurture will easily drive someone close to insanity if their child's life is unfortunately lost and it can drive someone to take another person's life to protect their child at the same time.

When I think about being a parent, I think about the awesome responsibility that the job has and in my case I have two young lives both younger than four that I am responsible for. This is where I start to think about how my father could miss out on these moments with me. Did he not feel the same emotions that I felt when I saw my boys being born? Did he not feel the same overwhelming waves of happiness when he looked into my eyes and I looked back at him for the first time?

How can a person walk away from something like that? I will cherish those memories for the rest of my life and I cannot fathom how he could remove himself from my life so easily. My love for my boys is so strong that I would run through a field of razors to get to one of them if they needed me. You see, right there; that desire is something that I assumed all parents have. My mother does, I know of other parents that share that sentiment. Yet, I don't know why my own father does not have that desire.

Maybe after reading this he can share his side of the story with me? Maybe he can explain this to me, I don't know how well I would receive what he says and I'm not sure if that situation will ever be possible. Why? The reason why is because my children have never met him. They have never seen him and they have no concept of who he is. That is why.

Back-story: when my first child was born we sent out birth announcements to all family and friends including my father. I was shocked to see that the announcement was sent back to me and I did not know how to deal with that. Even though we have been estranged for several years my father was invited to my wedding in 2008, and I have since seen him most recently at my grandmother's funeral in January 2012. My wife and I had two boys in the last three years and they don't know who he is.

Prior to our second son being born I decided not to send my father a birth announcement because I did not want to have that sent back to me as well. Here's the rub; I felt that in sending back the announcements and not attempting to "make things right" and use the opportunity of new life to potentially repair our relationship, my father was rejecting me and my children at the same time.....again. Oh no!.......I'm getting that feeling again. That "little box" may have been emptied of the pain but the anger was still lingering. I was on fire once again on the inside.

However, this time was different. I could not get into the anger and really roll around in it like I used to. The anger was fleeting and very inconsistent, which was very different from before. I could not get it to fester in my mind like I used to. I don't know if this is because I had two babies to distract me but my heart was handling this anger in a different way. I felt I was starting to change for the better. I started to feel like "okay yeah whatever" and that is different for me especially because I have been so concerned about his lack of involvement in my life prior to my children being born. So now what? I have to move on. I can't wait for someone to want to be a father and a grandfather. So I decided to stop expecting him to want to be a part of my boy's life. Judge me if you want, I don't give a damn. I think this is the best way for me to deal with things going forward. I'm not saying that he cannot be a part of my children's life but we would have to have months of major conversations before that would be able to happen. No, the children are not tools for me to use to make him be a father to me, but I will not allow him to pull a David Copperfield and disappear from their lives like he did with mine. I simply will not allow it.

Once again, judge me if you must, I don't…well you know what I'm about to say. When I think of the disappointment that I felt when my father did not follow up on a promise or when I could not find him I cannot imagine my boys going through that. No. Not going to happen again. So I am fine with him not even being mentioned. It's a terrible thing to do and I truly hate that I have to do that but my reasons are justified and it's happened too many times to think that the behavior is going to change, especially after the birth announcement deal.

What am I going to do when my children ask me about my father? I don't know. Well, I have to be honest with them, and the truth is when I was staying with him he was awesome, and I always wanted that from him. The rest of the time during his absence things were terrible. He has never mistreated me (yelled at me, anything like that) he was just not around. That is the truth. He is a good man, he has plenty of friends that care for him and a wife and step family that loves him as well. Oh and my family is over there in the corner too, by the way.

So it's really on me, JL, and my wife's father to teach these boys how to be men and I have to teach them how to be a Harden. However, I have to understand what that means. As a whole, my family is very strong. The Hardens are mainly out of the Midwest with some southern ties. We are strong and confident people with a universal tenacity that can get us in trouble at times. But that strong attitude and determination makes us great. We hustle; there is no such thing as a lazy Harden.

That is one of the traits that I love about my family as a whole. We will fight each other but we will all come together as a hive and kick your ass at the same time. I love it. Then there's the Harden temper, we all have it and managing it is essential to having the ability to fight another day without learning the harsh lessons that life provides us when we loose control and make poor decisions. I want my sons to have a relationship with their extremely large extended family. I am aware that some of my family members are in close contact with my father and I have to find a way to deal with that. To keep my children isolated from the rest of my family is stupid, and to do anything like that would be petty on my part. Sure some of them don't know or understand the scope of my relationship with my father and I can't expect them to. I'd only ask them to be as understanding as possible when talking to me about it. I don't want to get mad with them when discussing the issue and I feel like I owe them an explanation but this time I can't just say "don't judge me because....".

So am I afraid of what my family is going to think of me when they read this? Hell yeah. I don't know what they are going to say after reading this. I'm also concerned about what they are going to think about my father. Keep in mind my intent is to share my story with other children of divorce and single mothers with boys that are going through the same thing.

My goal is to share my experiences growing up without my father in my life. *I never wanted to intentionally hurt my father in writing this.* That being said, this may create some additional division in my family and I have to accept that. The thing is, I can't be worried about that. I have to get this out of my head because after I finish writing this book I am letting all of this go.

I don't want to hold on to any residual ager, no more pain, and I even want to let go of the memories. I want to devote my complete focus for the rest of my life to the success of my family and my marriage. Period. This is it, no more looking back, no regrets.

Here and Now

That last bit was difficult for me to write. Obviously, that was real and maybe my father will read it. But here is the thing, even if he doesn't, I feel better. When I look back at my life and think about where I am now I am proud of what I have accomplished. I am proud of the man that I have become. This written experience of my journey to understand who I am was worth the effort and time in writing all of this to you. I was concerned that you may think that I was a hypocrite for being angry with my father. No one likes rejection but his lack of interest in my children was to me the ultimate slap in the face. They say children don't come with instructions and that is the truth. I desperately want mine to have a childhood that is free of the stress and pain that I had.

However, I can't focus on that now, I have to focus on my own goals and this book is one of many. If you are a teenager and you have a parent that is not a part of your life, I hope you know now how to deal with your pain and emotions. It won't happen overnight but you will get through the pain. If you are an adult and never dealt with your pain, now you know what steps you have to take in order work out your feelings and deal with your pain. For me, I've learned by talking to you that I am okay. I am okay with the man that I am, I am okay with the life that I have, and I am okay with my family.

There is a saying that goes, "freedom isn't really free." What do you think being free means? For me, freedom comes in two forms: one being financially free to do what you want to do. This requires serious planning, tons of favor from God, and good decision-making. The second form of freedom is in your mind. What I mean by that is, by holding on to things from your past you are not free of it. To be truly free of something you have to not care about it anymore. This is very hard to do.

The main idea is this: Change how you see things. Your life is yours and you have to make the most of what you have. Focusing on the past will not change your future. Sounds cliché but it is the truth. *Your eyes may give you sight but your mind and soul provides you with vision.* This concept is something that I did not completely understand until I started this written conversation with you. Peace of mind is priceless and having a healthy sense of who you are is the ultimate form of freedom. Think about that, peace of mind, it's a profound statement. I really did not have peace of mind regarding my relationship with my father. I put aside dealing with my feelings for years due to my increasingly complex life. To be honest, my peace of mind is coming to me right now. No ink needed anymore, I'm fine the way I am.

In fact, it's my turn to be copied. I have two boys that need me and when it is time I'll be there for them when they are ready to push the "copy" button. Lastly, I pray that my words reach someone who knows someone who has a friend that *needs* a friend to read this book. This experience has changed me forever and I hope that my words help you and people that you love. Share this with those that need it. Thank you.

www.ingramcontent.com/pod-product-compliance
Lightning Source LLC
Chambersburg PA
CBHW060947040426
42445CB00011B/1036